The Gratitude Response

FIND TRUE HAPPINESS

TONY BRADY

DEDICATION

For Fran, Paul, Bonnie and Jayden
May you each find Happiness through Gratitude

ACKNOWLEDGMENTS

I wish to thank the following people for their inspiration which led to the creation of this book:

My wife Fran for her patience and her endless encouragement. Fortunately for me Fran sees nothing as impossible.

The members of the Open Heart Sangha in Dublin, the members of Mindfulness Meditation Dublin Meetup and the contributors to and members of the inspiring Insight Timer Meditation App.

The minister Rev. Bridget Spain, former minister Rev. Bill Darlison and my friends in the Dublin Unitarian Church whose openness to ideas from all sources has been a constant source of inspiration to me over the years.

It goes without saying that none of this would have been possible without all the inspirational ideas I have come across through the years in a whole library of writings and podcasts on the subjects of meditation and mindfulness.

I am very grateful to each and every one of you.

Tony Brady – Dublin – 16 May 2016

CONTENTS

INTRODUCTION

The idea for this book came about as a result of my discovery of Naikan, a Japanese practice of self-reflection based on three questions:

What have I received from others?
What have I given to others?
What difficulties or trouble have I caused others?

My introduction to this life-changing practice was simply through my good fortune to come across an on-line retreat given by Gregg Krech and listed among the impressive selection of on-line retreat resources available at www.tricycle.org.

I have sincerely tried, as very many of us have, to practice the virtue of thankfulness. I honestly believe I did not take the good things of life for granted. However, listening to Gregg amplified dramatically my awareness of the inundation of benefits which flow to each one of us every single minute of every day.

Setting out these events in the form of a balance sheet and comparing the benefits coming in with the paucity of what is going out is a sobering discovery. It encouraged me to look more carefully around and observe above, below, to my right and to my left, an endless source of benefits previously taken for granted. It made me realise that the world owes me nothing at all. Indeed, I am heavily indebted to the world and its people.

In the journey of life, we resemble explorers working our way through a thick forest where everything we come across is benefit upon benefit upon benefit. But with eyes closed we press on unthinkingly, believing these things to be obstacle upon obstacle. We slash and we complain as we try to fight our way blindly through what we perceive to be dense, menacing undergrowth. With the practice of gratitude we can open our eyes and see the world and the people around us in a new light, in their right light, and that light invites us to be grateful.

May the daily practice of gratitude bring you the reward of true happiness every day of your life.

Tony Brady - Dublin - 16 May 2016

"If the only prayer you ever say in your entire life is thank you, it will be enough"

- Meister Eckhart

WAKING UP

We wake up each morning and mostly we feel fine. We open our eyes; we hear the first sounds of the day. We stretch, emerge from a warm bed to a warm room, visit the bathroom for a morning pee. We flush the toilet, find clean water on tap, wash, clean our teeth, dress, enter the kitchen, press a switch, make a cup of tea or coffee, have breakfast.

What we receive and what we give in life are like entries in a bank account. We look at the extent of today's income with amazement and we see little or no outgoings. It makes us realise that the world owes us nothing, it is we who owe so much to the world. Can we try today to reduce the credit balance appearing in the account books of our lives?

This everyday morning ritual provides us with an ideal opportunity to notice the benefits that we so often take for granted. We have family, friends, rest and shelter and the comforts of home. We enjoy light and heat, drinking water, sanitation, clothing, footwear. We have food for breakfast, refrigeration, power, and all this before we have scarcely begun the day. Have we even noticed the air that we breathe? Have we been aware of our lungs working through the night without any intervention on our part, just one of the frequently overlooked wonders bringing us to the gift of this new day?

If we could open our eyes to the simple things that every new morning unfailingly brings, it would inform our attitude and it would affect for the better our relationship with the people we meet in the course of the day. An attitude of gratitude is a positive start to any day and a beneficial focus in any life.

Instead of complaining when the breakfast cereal runs out we would benefit greatly by reminding ourselves of the many days when the supply does not run out. Just consider for a moment where our breakfast has come from before it reaches us. Think of the ingredients, the planting, the careful cultivation, harvesting, packaging and transporting of this everyday commodity before it finally lands on a supermarket shelf where we select it from an astounding variety of different possibilities offered to us in this amazingly beneficent world.

Reflect for a moment on all the people whose dedicated and cooperative work has been involved in bringing this first meal of the day to us. Not only have we the cereal but we have it packed with the benefit of quality control standards, "best before date" calculated, vitamin content shown and dietary advice offered on the box. Very often we mindlessly eat this breakfast, the product of so much labour and so much loving effort on the part of so many people. It can even be munched on the hoof as we direct our attention to the TV, read the newspaper, absorb ourselves in our electronic devices and all the while planning "other things to be done".

Many people believe in God while others do not. But whatever our attempt at understanding this wondrous reality in which we live and move and have our being, this awakening to a new day and the receipt of such benefit, even before the day's work begins, is a cause for pause, a reason for profound thankfulness and a basis for constant gratitude.

We might usefully turn around a phrase of G. K. Chesterton and exclaim "Here begins a new day. Yesterday I had eyes, ears, hands and the great world around me. Why am I allowed yet another day?" Why indeed?

In a sentence or two:
Hey, I am awake again, a new day lies ahead of me.

The Gratitude Response:
What will I do with this amazing new day, how will I spend the next 24 hours of my life?

THE ASTONISHING HUMAN BODY

It is both humbling and constructive for each of us to pause for a fresh look at the body which we take so much for granted. We each have had this extraordinary and complex human form since our earliest moment of existence and we use it, unthinkingly most of the time, until we notice that some taken-for-granted body parts fail to perform as usual. Our bodies are in a constant state of renewal and replacement. Cells die and the body replaces them all the time without any intervention on our part, and yet through all this we retain an individual identity even as our ideas and personalities mature and change over time.

We need to express gratitude for our limbs, our senses, our brain, our lungs, our heart and internal organs. We need to give thanks for the fact that we breathe, hear, see, smell, touch.

The brain is the most complex structure known to humankind. The workings of the human brain and its relationship to the astonishing facts and mysteries of mind and consciousness remain to be understood. This relatively small organ, which we can easily hold in one hand, has the most extraordinary number of interconnections compared to which even the most advanced and intricate of our computer systems bear no comparison whatsoever. We have gifts of intelligence, personal identity, wisdom, memory, feelings, all of which arise from the fact that we each carry within our skulls this astonishing small organ which directs all our physical and mental processes.

From our first moments of life until our last, our hearts beat without rest and yet we exercise no control whatever over this life-sustaining activity. This regular beating is something of which we are blissfully oblivious except when it occasionally goes out of sync. When that happens it brings us into a sudden frighteningly sharp awareness of our very tenuous grip on life. Then our attention is drawn to the startling realisation that our very existence from second to second depends on upon this hardworking never-resting organ which maintains our intricate circulatory system.

Our lungs provide us with life-sustaining oxygen without which we would expire within minutes. Unless we make a conscious decision to pay attention to our breath, this activity proceeds on auto-pilot almost entirely unnoticed by us.

We have limbs, our legs which enable us to move around, our arms and hands with which we can grasp and manipulate objects. We rarely have to think about how we need to contract our muscles and move our limbs as we go about the business of the day.

Our eyes are a marvel of evolutionary design through which we can distinguish a vast array of colours, shades and textures. When these hardworking organs require support, we have the benefit of sight adjusting spectacles, contact lenses and, more recently, laser surgery to help us on our way.

Thanks to our ears we have the ability to communicate and co-operate with each other. Our ears enable us to enjoy the gift of music; they facilitate the development of language, discussion, and learning. They give us our priceless ability to pass information from person to person and from generation to generation in understandable ways which allow for the accumulation of knowledge and the sharing of ideas and experiences.

Our senses of smell and taste empower us to recognise scents and flavours and they make our food appetising. These senses enable us to distinguish between which offerings might be edible and nutritious and which may not be so good or might even be be dangerous to eat.

Our immune system fights off infections and diseases, our digestive system converts our food into energy and permits the body to repair itself; our blood conveniently clots when we cut ourselves, all this activity taking place within a self-regulating temperature control system the external evidence of which we observe as normal sweating.

In every corner of our bodies, we have un-noticed organs which work to hold us in a balanced equilibrium which it is far beyond our ability to replicate artificially.

The human body is a marvel of evolution and engineering. Consider the obstacles encountered when our most capable scientists and inventors attempt to programme robots to perform a variety of the simplest of human tasks. We stand in awe and wonder at the thought of how each of us can relate to our environment and, even without thinking, manage to go about all the diverse business of the day. Single purpose robots have been developed and are phenomenally successful in certain industries, for example in manufacturing, including car manufacturing, where they can out-perform human beings in the carrying out of repetitive tasks. But when you move beyond these straightforward and standardised functions and attempt to create machines to perform a variety of tasks requiring manual dexterity, the fantastic and extraordinarily varied nature of our human abilities is swiftly brought back to mind.

In a sentence or two:
Today, actually pay attention to your body, consider all its working parts. See if you can notice the few (if any) parts of your amazing body that are giving you any trouble at all.

The Gratitude Response:
Realise that this good health is not permanent and therefore be thankful, especially on what are clearly the good and trouble free days.

THE BATHROOM

Consider how we can take for granted the fact that we have a bathroom in our house or apartment. Very many people, even today, do not enjoy that comfort. In reasonably prosperous societies it is not uncommon to have two or more bathrooms. Some people have bathrooms for every occupant of a house and some homeowners can even boast (if that be the right word) of their houses having more bathrooms than occupants.

In a bathroom, we have the privacy of our personal washing and toilet space. We have lighting, mirrors, ventilation, heating, a space for hand towels, face towels, bath towels, shelves for all the variety of lotions, creams and potions that we have stored, ready to be applied before we present ourselves to the outside world.

Here you will find shaving gear, pre-shaving lotions, shaving foams, gels, creams, oils, razors and razor blades, aftershave lotions; all that men require for modern male grooming.

You will find shelves stocked with products designed to help protect us before we face the sun. Sun creams and blocks of various factors, each devised to match particular skin types, creams and sprays to be applied before, during and after exposure to the light of day.

How we smell to others is a matter of some importance and considerable worry to many. So to minimise the possibility of people around us detecting real body odours we have, ready for application, a variety of soaps, perfumes, sprays, applicators and roll-on devices in a vast range of scents.

For our teeth, we have at least one toothbrush each (probably many more) electric and battery operated toothbrushes, toothpicks, flossers, and dental mirrors. We have toothpaste of great diversity, usually a different variety to match the multiplicity of tastes and needs of each occupant of the house, especially the current desire to appear in front of others with nothing less than a sparkling white smile.

The bathroom is in many cases tiled and heated and we have baths, traditional and Jacuzzi, showers, manual and electric, powered or gravity fed, stand alone or over bath. Wet rooms save even the fit and athletic among us the inconvenience of having to lift or bend our legs in order to enter the shower area. For many people, the former humble bathroom has become a recreation area, a private spa with atmospheric lighting, candles and mood music to add to the comforts which people in the prosperous north and west of the world have come to expect in the early part of the 21st century.

These descriptions of excess are not designed to make us feel bad at the good fortune some may possess by having all of these conveniences, indeed many of us are very happy with much less.

The purpose is to draw attention to even the simplest of our bathrooms, notice the extraordinary good fortune represented by each and every one of the contents of this littlest of our household rooms, formerly referred to as a water closet. It encourages us to express thanks for all that we have.

Familiarity is said to breed contempt and while the majority of us may not feel scorn as we enter into our little private space for daily cleansing, the question is whether we notice the abundance with which we are blessed every day by the presence of all the usual toiletries and conveniences which we find "just there".

A great many of these benefits, even the very bathroom itself, are not "just there" for quite a large percentage of the population of the planet. By raising our awareness of the many things which fill our lives, may we be inspired to share our extraordinary good fortune with those who are much worse off than we are ourselves.

In a sentence or two:
When next you visit your bathroom, just take a second or two to notice your good fortune, observe how you are standing in an amazing little space the likes of which would have been unknown to earlier generations.

The Gratitude Response:
Consider twinning your toilet. You can help people in desperate poverty to have access to a proper toilet, clean water and advice which they need in order to remain healthy. See www.toilettwinning.org.

GETTING DRESSED

We sleepily reach into our wardrobes, or in some cases slip into a dressing room. Here we find a selection of clothes offering us different possibilities for presenting our desired image of the day to the outside world.

Notice for a minute or two the creaking shelves and the compressed state of the rails. Examine the used, the under-used and the unused clothes, the winter clothes and the summer clothes, the inner wear and the outerwear. Notice the formal wear and the casual wear, the jeans and the chinos, the long dresses, short dresses, holiday gear, rain gear. Examine the walking shoes, casual shoes, city shoes, high heels, low heels, medium heels, climbing boots, slippers, all with many duplicates in a kaleidoscope of colours and shapes. There might even be, among this collection and assortment, party pieces for special occasions, fancy dress outfits, Santa Claus suits, scary costumes for Halloween and, for married people, a once used bridal dress.

In these wardrobes and shelves, we will find items that we have not worn for years, mementos of our earlier thinner, fatter or younger selves, each of them a reminder of the quickly passing years with their short-lived fads and their ever changing fashions. We have clothes that ought to have been donated to charity long ago. We have hoarded clothes that we believe might come in useful "someday" even if only for work about the house or the garden.

All this reminds us that life has blessed us with abundance. We think with gratitude of how we had the health, wisdom and good fortune to be able to earn money so that we could buy each of these items. We recall the excitement of anticipation and selection; the enjoyment experienced at the time of each new purchase. We also notice the sobering effect of the swift passing of time, a reminder of constant change, the fading of interest coming about as quickly and surely as the fading of the clothes themselves.

Looking into our wardrobes and shelves should prompt a thought for the people and processes involved in bringing the contents of these wardrobes to us. Our decision to buy any product is not a stand-alone act. Every purchase has an effect upon others. Is the item ethically produced? Is it manufactured with the aid of an objectionable working process, something akin to child labour or virtual slave labour? Has the item been transported across the planet? Price is an important consideration for many of us but even paying a higher price offers no guarantee that what we are buying is fairly produced so we must exercise caution when shopping for clothes. And we must pay attention to the quality of the goods which we decide to purchase. The manufacture of each item has an impact on the environment and it is not to our credit to add to the mounting problems of the planet by encouraging the fabrication of poor quality short-lived items which will all too soon be cast aside as useless.

In a consumerist society where people are the targets of constant advertising, we also have to ask ourselves if this proposed purchase is truly necessary. Looking again at our creaking shelves and bulging wardrobes can we, for today at least, say with some sincerity "Thank you, but I have more than enough already."

People today enjoy an abundance which their ancestors would have found unthinkable a few short generations ago. For what we have, let us be truly grateful. Our bounty can be noticed and acknowledged each day when we reach into our wardrobes. The simple act of selecting and putting on our clothes can be a practice in mindful living and an exercise in gratitude.

In a sentence or two:
Looking into your wardrobe, how often have you thought "Look at this state of this wardrobe, how is it that can it be so full and I still believe I cannot find anything to wear?"

The Gratitude Response:
Look more closely, donate your excess to some worthy cause. How long has something to lie here unused before you decide to pass it on to someone else who needs it and will be happy to make use of it?

BREAKFAST TIME

We relax and enjoy the first meal of the day. Not for us the simple fare of bygone years which kept our parents and grandparents more than satisfied. Today we are invited to start the day with an unprecedented variety of breakfast possibilities from all over the world.

A visit, even to a small supermarket, will present us with offerings which could have our palates exploring new tastes for quite a long time. Visit a larger store and, even for breakfast you will find an array of morning offerings which is daunting in variety. Think of the generic term "breakfast cereal". In the space allocated to these, you will see laid out in row after row and shelf upon shelf a miracle of production and distribution that is amazing to contemplate.

Moving on through the rows in search of "tea" and, as well as traditional tea, you will see teas of every conceivable description, fruit tea of every flavour, white tea, green tea, all types of exotic infusions. You will meet herbal teas, aromatic and calming teas, medicinal teas, tea in leaf form, tea bags, caffeinated tea, decaffeinated tea; the list goes on and on. Nearby you will see coffee offered in as many genres and varieties. The world has become a small place indeed and widespread and cheaper travel has resulted in all of our taste buds having become global in character.

There was a time when bread was simply white bread or brown bread but that was long ago. Today you are offered a choice of seeded or unseeded bread, soda bread, whole-meal bread, thick sliced bread, thin sliced bread, sesame seed bread, poppy seed bread, banana bread, tomato bread. The staff of life can be home-made or factory produced and it comes in an unprecedented variety of forms and shapes, rolls, pita bread, bagels, wraps. It must easily be possible to work your way through different samples of today's unprecedented varieties of bread for a year without ever tasting the same type twice.

These are only a small fraction of the offerings which present themselves to us for our breakfast. Fresh fruit is available in season and out of season from almost any part of this ever more interconnected world. It can be accompanied by an unprecedented selection of yoghurts and creams and spreads to match our every mood.

All of this variety prompts a need to express gratitude. It can be difficult navigating the well-stocked aisles of our ultra-modern mega-supermarkets. Impatience and tiredness can often be our predominant feelings as we go about our weekly shopping expedition. However, in all fairness, we need to stop now and then, look around and realise what an exceptional gift it is to be on the receiving end of such abundance.

These varied offerings carry with them obligations as well. Never has food travelled so far from farm to table. It is unsustainable to refrigerate and transport food across the globe when the same could be sourced closer to home. We have to ask if it is reasonable in, for example, the northern hemisphere to expect fresh strawberries on our tables on Christmas Day. In a world where poverty is rife and resources finite we have an obligation and a duty to act more responsibly and more ethically. Future generations of social commentators will look upon our time as a period of super production and superabundance. But they will also see our time as a time of reckless disregard for generations yet unborn, people who will have to live or die with the consequences of our daily choices, including the choices which we make when selecting our breakfast cereals. We have so much for which we must be grateful but we must also remember our parallel responsibility to those who have little or nothing and to the people who will come after us.

In a sentence or two:
When shopping and eating try to remember what effort and energy, love and care, has gone into the bringing of this food to you and see if you can shop for food that will lessen your footprint on the environment.

The Gratitude Response:
Be grateful for every bite of food remembering that the food on your table is a gift of the whole universe. Food ought to be available to all. Offer support to charities which help people

who do not have enough to eat. Only buy what you need and never throw out good food. Bring a doggy bag when you go out

for a meal (You know how often people in restaurants receive more than they need) Encourage your government to follow the progressive example of France and Italy where legislation has been introduced prohibiting stores from throwing away or destroying unsold food.

THE HUMBLE TELEPHONE

Before leaving home, we may need to make a telephone call. This now everyday task introduces us to one of the world's unnoticed miracles. You lift a little instrument, dial in a number and without further thought, you are connected to someone across the world. If each of us has a smart device, we can even see the other person as we speak. Indeed, if we had the need to make contact, we could speak to and see an astronaut circling the earth on the International Space Station.

In the late 19th century telephony was in its infancy. From a situation where we had telephone lines individually connected between subscribers we have moved through stages of, initially manual, then automatic telephone exchanges, and on to today and the almost universal availability of telephone devices. In was only in the 1970s that mobile phones appeared on the scene, initially expensive, unwieldy and cumbersome devices with limited standby and usage time, long recharging times, and available to, and used by, only a tiny and relatively wealthy minority of people. Mobile phones have become cheaper, smaller, and more powerful. In an unimaginable development of the technology, their use today has extended vastly beyond their initial purpose of facilitating something as basic as the making of a simple telephone connection, albeit on the move. Today's average smartphone is much more than a simple call-making and call-receiving machine, it is quite a powerful, albeit a tiny, computer.

We live in a world where a vast number of people have never experienced life without a mobile phone, or even for that matter, life without a fixed telephone line. In such a world it is understandable that we fail to give thanks for the miracle lying before us on the table or sitting so lightly in our pockets. Indeed, the almost universal availability of the telephone has made us imagine that we have an inalienable right to be able to make contact without fail with anyone at all wherever and whenever we please. Notice the frustration which tends to arise when you lift the phone, press the connect button and find that nothing happens. "What is the matter with this phone provider, this is the second time I have been offline in the last week. I tell you I am going to have to give them a piece of my mind, terminate the contract and move to a provider who will offer a reliable phone service" Memories, like gratitude, can be short-lived.

Is it not that case that what is considered a miracle by one generation is routine to the next and a museum exhibit soon after that? I remember the surprise, not to mention shock, I felt when I saw a golf ball typewriter, the height of technology at one point in my life, sitting alongside old bits and pieces in a country museum after what seemed to me to be only a few short years.

Thankfulness can be transitory; gratefulness can be absent and we do not notice the things (nor even the people) whose presence enable life for us to go on as easily and as comfortably as it does. Admittedly we are, generally speaking, more appreciative of unusual new gifts, such as the first acquisition of a new phone or the first performance of a good deed by a new person. But after a while, we take the regular and the reliable for granted and we drift into a pattern of expectancy where the standard and the constant become an unnoticed and unappreciated part of our everyday life.

Perhaps when we next reach for what has become quite a conventional mobile telephone to make or receive a call, to send a text, check the weather, the news, the maps, the music or book a ticket we might first stop and pay attention to how wonderful this is. When we lift the same device to check our emails, Skype a friend on the other side of the earth, ask Google for information or set out to do any one of the hundred and one other things that a "phone" can now do, we might just pause and give thanks. Wait, even for a second or two, look at the little miracle resting so comfortably in our hand and, in our own minds, utter some words expressing amazement.

Albert Einstein captured the idea perfectly when, in his work "Everything is a Miracle" he referred to the fact that there are only two ways to live your life. One is as though nothing is a miracle. The other is as though everything is a miracle.

In a sentence or two:

Try to imagine life without a telephone. Consider even the mild inconvenience of having to go to a phone box (yes there was a time when there were such structures set up on the streets) to make a phone call, imagine your car suffering a mechanical breakdown on the road without your having the ability to sit comfortably in the vehicle as you telephone for assistance.

The Gratitude Response:

Be thankful rather than frustrated or anxious when you hear the phone ring, take a brief moment for reflection before you make or answer a call. Each time you use the phone remember that you are dealing with a real person, someone just like you. Yes, notice that someone just like you, someone with the same hopes and dreams and fears is speaking to you on the other end of the line and treat that person just as you would like to be treated yourself.

GETTING THROUGH THE DAY

With early morning tasks complete, and early morning benefits received, we head off to work, school or college.

We might find it useful to pay attention to what we encounter along the way, transport of some description, public or private transport or the ability to walk. Remember the fact that we have an educational establishment or a workplace to go to, and all the many benefits that either of these institutions offers us.

In school, we have the support of teachers and friends, access to books and the accumulated knowledge which dwells in them. We have teachers who have studied their art and skill, people expert in their subjects, educators who have dedicated a substantial part of their lives to the transmission of knowledge, ideas and ideals to others.

Any educational institution requires a huge support system, first of all, staff, vision, then premises and grounds, classrooms and furniture, funding, curriculum and educational programmes, technology, record keeping, procedures for the maintenance of discipline, systems for liaising with parents, support systems for people with specific needs. A superficial visit to any such establishment on any one day will show only a little of the nature and extent of the people and the physical support systems that are required to be sitting in place before we even enter a school or college gate.

When we go to work, we are equally the recipients of a marvellous array of taken-for-granted benefits starting with the fact of having any work to go to at all. We may be self-employed but it does not follow that we are self-sufficient and independent of the needs and even the whims of our customers or clients. Without people who require our services or the goods we provide, we would have no work. In many instances, our employment will involve our being a co-operative part of a much larger group of people working for an institution of one kind or another. That entity had to be established by someone or some group of individuals who had the imagination, vision, foresight and financial means to launch it on its way. Just step back, take a look at the workplace and note the people who are part of it. Look at the premises, the equipment, the external services, the many and varied, large and small components without which the organisation would cease to be. We are all part of an extremely interdependent web of existence.

With the day's work done, we have the gift of a place we call home, the opportunity for recreation and relaxation, a place where we can be ourselves, our little corner of the world.

Finally, we fall into bed, a comfort not universally enjoyed. We have peace, security, warmth; all provided thanks to a host of people mostly unknown to us, but without whose co-operation and support our lives as we experience them would be impossible.

Every day of our existence provides us with so many reasons to be thankful, so many reasons why we might feel an obligation to pay back something to people and to the world in general. We mostly find a significant discrepancy between the credit and debit sides of the account books of our lives. Mindful reflection each evening may provide the inspiration for us to try to bring these accounts nearer to a position of balance.

In a sentence or two:
Notice and be grateful for some of the many people and the services that support your daily life and think how much more awkward it would be for you if you were to try to manage without this assistance.

The Gratitude Response:
Be ready to offer sincere thanks. If you only stop and think, you will notice that you have very many reasons to express gratitude every day of your life.

THE AMAZING YOU

Before we move on to consider the wider world and the people who inhabit it, we must spend a little time thinking about the miracle that is the life and the existence of each one of us.

Most people now accept that the universe which we inhabit today had its beginnings in a moment which is called the Big Bang, an event of unimaginable magnitude which scientists believe took place some 13.7 billion years ago. Astronomical observations offer proof that the universe is expanding. Just as in the world of sound, the Doppler Effect produces a change of pitch according to whether the object emitting the sound, for example, an ambulance, is approaching the listener, or receding, the colour of an astronomical object will change according to whether it is moving towards or away from the observer. These observations prove that the latter is the case, the universe is expanding in all directions. It follows therefore that at some point in the very distant past the entire of the cosmos must necessarily have been compressed into a space of unimaginable density.

Over the billions of years since the Big Bang, a situation finally developed where our solar system and its planets, including the Earth, took shape. First simple, and then more complex life forms evolved, ultimately developing into the intelligent, reflective species which we have finally become.

We next have to go on to consider our parents, grandparents, our great grandparents. When we look at the statistical odds involving that series of individuals and then consider the fact of you or I having come into existence, we are in awe that, despite the incalculable odds, we are here, living, thinking conscious beings. We are suspended in a fleeting instant, appearing in what is little more than a momentary flash of time, positioned somewhere between eternity and infinity. Words fail when attempting to describe the extraordinary phenomenon that is our existence. For millennia, since time and thought first emerged, people have pondered answerless questions concerning this amazing reality, "why?", "how come?", "for what reason?" "in what circumstances?". The questions are never-ending as the answers are elusive.

Religious systems and philosophies try to make sense of the fact, some in absolute terms which conflict with our notions of common sense. How may beings such as we are, finite in time and limited in our ever expanding notions of time and space, make other than the feeblest attempt to explain humanity's place in an incomprehensibly vast universe? Indeed, some scientists now believe ours may just be one of many universes and the entire of which might well be limitless in both time and space. In all this, we are simply like ants trying to understand the solar system.

But still there is one feeling which must fill the hearts of all thinking people, anyone who has ever looked into the eyes of a new-born child, anyone who has ever gazed up into the night sky. It is a feeling of awe and wonder and gratitude. It may indeed prove impossible for any of us ever to comprehend the reason why we are here, but let us just reflect on the reality that we are in fact here now and express sincere and profound thanks for that fact.

By any definition, our individual existence is a miracle, a wonder, a marvel, a phenomenon, a cause justifying endless gratitude and thankfulness, a justification for appreciation. It imposes on us an obligation to make a difference in the world and a responsibility to the people around us. It imposes on us a duty of trust in caring for the planet we inhabit, a commitment to the beings with whom we share this floating piece of rock upon which we make our annual trip around our life-giving sun.

Mary Oliver puts a profound question to us in her poem "The Summer Day" when she asks "Tell me, what is it you plan to do with your one wild and precious life?"
The phenomenon of our existence leaves us with a need to answer the same question. It calls for an answer born of a spirit of childlike wonder and enduring gratefulness.

In a sentence or two:

Can you find time to stop and reflect on your existence and come to realise that the life of every one of us is truly miraculous?

The Gratitude Response:

Today, pause for a while. Stop for a moment and honestly try to notice the gift of your being here and be genuinely thankful for that extraordinary fact.

THINGS ABOUT THE HOUSE

Let's take a look at and around the place where we live and try to pay attention to the variety of goods and services which we barely notice and for which we ought to be thankful.

There is first of all the physical structure of our buildings, the foundations, walls, ceilings and roof. Consider for a moment the source of these materials, the skill and work of the people involved in planning the places we call home and the work of finally assembling the pieces into the shape we recognise as home.

Some of the material for our homes, bricks, stone, metal, concrete, glass, cement, slate, will have come from sources situated a very long distance from the final building, much of the material from locations abroad from where it had to be transported by land air or sea. We cannot even begin to calculate or imagine the complex web of co-operation involved in bringing together the necessary materials for even the simplest building. Do we ever think to give this a second thought as we turn the key in the door when we arrive home?

Apart from its basic structure a home comprises and contains an extraordinary number and variety of services connecting it to the outside world, lighting, heating, ventilation, water and sewage systems, telecommunications. In some cases, we are even fortunate to have smart homes the services to which can be accessed and programmed remotely. Internally the homes of the 21st century are equipped with appliances and devices which would have been beyond the wildest dreams of the most fortunate and even the most imaginative members of society only a few short years ago. We live in the midst of the stuff of science fiction.

Our time has endowed us with labour saving devices which defy listing and which make easy work of jobs which formerly occupied a great deal of our available time. This abundance has been a mixed blessing for many people. Clearly, anything which avoids people having to spend their days doing mechanical, tiresome and repetitive work is something to be applauded. But in our search for ever more labour saving devices, we have at times become slaves to our machines and slaves to the ever lengthening work schedules that we have to maintain in order to pay for these mechanical supports. Sometimes we might find it a blessing and a source of gratitude to practice "doing without".

In expressing thankfulness for all the benefits of home, we have to be aware of the countless millions of people in the world, even today, who do not have a place which they can call home. There are those who have never had a permanent building in which to live and there are millions who have been displaced by war, famine, drought and disease. We can truthfully say "there but for fortune go you or I". In our abundance, we must actively work to ease the pain of others. If we fail to do so as individuals and communities, then our very abundance will be an indictment of our lives and of our time. Our abundance calls for real gratitude. Genuine gratitude must involve mindfully reflecting upon our wealth as compared with the poverty of others. That careful reflection must result in real action to try to make this world a more equitable place for all its people.

In a sentence or two:
Pay attention to all that goes to make up the place you call home. Your home is more than a building but the building itself is the product of the hard work and effort of so many people whose identity will never be known to you.

The Gratitude Response:
Be grateful for what you have and be supportive of the very many people who do not enjoy the security of home. Think of individuals who are far from home, refugees from war and terror, people persecuted because of colour, race or religion. Think of people discriminated against because of their gender or their sexual orientation, people who are homeless and persecuted because of their beliefs.

PEOPLE IN OUR LIVES

None of us can logically attempt to claim an independent individual existence. Every minute of every day we are supported by the interconnected world around us and by the co-operative actions of countless people without whom life as we know and enjoy it would be an impossibility.

As babies, we are born into a situation of total dependence on the people around us. As we grow in wisdom and strength and learn to exercise our will and flex our muscles we can, for a time, become lost in an illusion of independence. We know what is best. We are fit and athletic. Life stretches endlessly before us and for many of us, it can take quite a while for the reality of interdependence to dawn. In our young days, we might, if we are lucky, be spared the sight or news of illness, be saved the pain of loss and death. For years, we can enjoy the gift of a life of carefree happiness in the innocence of a secure childhood.

As we advance in years, it is to be hoped that we can manage to retain something of that innocence and optimism of youth. As all of us grow to maturity, the reality of interdependence becomes clear to us and we come to appreciate that nothing, and no one, exists in an independent, self-sustaining bubble. We are part of a vast interdependent web of existence. "Pluck one thread, and the web ye mar; break but one of a thousand keys, and the paining jar through all will run," says John Greenleaf Whittier. 1808 - 1892.

Our lives are enhanced, even made possible at all, by the kindness and co-operation of countless people known to us and unknown. Obviously this group will comprise family and close friends, then neighbours, teachers, school and college friends, people for whom we work or individuals who work for us. We need the support of shopkeepers and traders, transport workers, cleaners and sanitation workers, communications people, civil servants, police and emergency workers, the list is as endless as the people are almost numberless.

An extraordinary feature of this superabundance is its mostly unfailing reliability to the point where we hardly notice all the work, effort and co-operation which is involved in allowing us to live our lives in the comfort and security to which we have become accustomed.

The kindnesses and co-operation of people near and far from us which facilitate our every action passes as unnoticed as the air which we breathe or the daylight which invites us to wakefulness each morning. It takes a stoppage, a weather event, an industrial dispute or something of the sort before we come to realise how much we depend upon the services of others. One day we press a switch and to our surprise we find the electricity has failed, we turn a tap and find only a trickle of water, we hear about an interruption to the transport system. These rare interruptions to our usual conveniences can be a source of irritation and can give rise to disproportionate feelings of annoyance and frustration. But if we approach life mindfully and in a spirit of gratitude we can use these occasional disruptions to our usual comfort as a basis of for heedful reflection on all many common benefits which come to us uninterruptedly day after day and which often go unnoticed.

This taking for granted of the regular things of life is a familiar experience. Perhaps it is well that it is so. In that way, it is a proof of our everyday superabundance. We seldom hear good news headlines. Kind deeds are rarely reported. It is re-assuring to see that the good and the decent actions of the vast majority of people are not so rare as to make the headlines.

In a sentence or two:
Whether we realise it or whether we fail to notice it, our lives as we live them day by day are lives of interdependence. We are all intimately connected with one another and the concern of one must be the concern of all.

The Gratitude Response:
Notice how much we depend on other people. Ask if we are as dependable as we might be? Are we as happy to give as to receive? Are we as comfortable offering help as asking for help? Take a look at the balance sheet of our life. Notice how much we have accumulated in the bank of life and consider how much we might be able to pay out.

PEOPLE AT OUR SERVICE

At some stage in our lives, each one of us has cause to visit a doctor or a reason be admitted to hospital. Even more frequently we will have need of dental services. When these occasions arise it might be helpful to recall that the benefits and treatments on offer have not always been so.

It would be unthinkable for people in the developed world today to consider undergoing a surgical operation, or even a dental procedure, without an anaesthetic or sedative of some sort. However only since the mid-1800's has such an aid been available. Before that, surgery, if required at all, was a horrifying and painful experience for the patient and a terrifying one even for the surgeon. Up to that point, reliance had to be placed on narcotics, alcohol and even the knocking out of the patient to minimise the pain and suffering that medical operations and dental treatment involved.

The development of medicine and the greater understanding of the workings of the human body which have taken place in the last 100 years almost defy belief. Medicines have been fine honed to deal with and cure a huge variety of illnesses and ailments. Diseases which were once rampant and the cause of widespread deaths have been eliminated or brought under reasonable control in many parts of the world. Vaccinations provide immunity against life-threatening illnesses by triggering the body to generate defences against a weaker version of the particular sickness. Surgery has become ever more sophisticated, enabling internal operations with the aid of tiny instruments which can be inserted into the body without any need for major incisions and openings.

Medical research and developments have given us the ability to transplant many organs including kidneys, liver, lungs, pancreas, intestines and even hearts. People with severe heart conditions can have bypass surgery; stents can be inserted to keep blood vessels open and, thanks to the invention of the pacemaker surgeons can now assist people who require support in order to regulate the heart rate.

We have sophisticated artificial limbs allowing people to walk again and replacement hips and knees are so commonplace as not to cause the raising of an eyebrow.

Assisted reproduction has aided many childless couples to have children. The first ever baby to be conceived in a test tube was born in 1978 but egg and sperm donation and in vitro fertilisation have become unexceptional in less than the following half century.

Diseases such as cancer which were once almost certain killers are now better understood and in a growing number of cases can be treated successfully by an ever increasingly sophisticated array of drugs and procedures.

A visit to a dentist, doctor or hospital is not something that anyone is likely to look forward to with enthusiasm, but when the occasion arises it is helpful to reflect on the wonders of medicine in our time and be grateful for all the possibilities and comfort that current medical procedures offer us. Provision of these services comes at a cost and sometime a heavy cost. In the developed world these opportunities for healthcare are available to us through taxation or through private medical care. But many places and many people lack necessary medical treatment because of lack of funds. This privation represents a failure of our efforts to cultivate a universal human vision and is a blot on our civilisation.

Organisations such as Médecins Sans Frontières (Doctors Without Borders) are an exceptional source of help to people who otherwise would be forced to go without essential medical aid. MSF currently works in almost 70 countries around the world, providing emergency medical care where the need is greatest.

Organisations such as MSF need our support, support which should be generously forthcoming as we look with gratitude upon our own good fortune when confronted with our medical needs.

In a sentence or two:

Just imagine having to seek medical or dental treatment in the "good old days". Stay with that awful thought for a while pending the arising of a feeling of gratitude.

The Gratitude Response:

Be grateful that you live in the 21st century with all its advantages. If you can afford to do so, please consider making a donation to organisations such as Médecins Sans Frontières.

THE MIRACLE OF BIRTH

Nowhere is our sense of awe, wonder and gratitude more keenly noticed than in the wonder of the life creation process, an everyday miracle. Modern science, medicine and photography have brought into daylight the secret workings of human reproduction. What was always a cause for thanksgiving has become a source of astonishment as our miniature cameras and probes explore, record and bring to light the inner recesses of the human reproductive system and allow us witness the very moment of the creation of a new human life.

Our cameras have exposed the human egg as it emerges from the ovary. We have seen the swirling mass of microscopic sperm as they swim and thrash their way towards their pre-programmed target. The very moment of conception has emerged from the dark recesses of mystery into the wonder of light and awareness. We have seen videos of the moment of human conception, seen the earliest human cells as they divide and subdivide, becoming in just a little time ever more human in appearance, an embryonic person floating in a life-sustaining womb and growing and developing day by day until the moment of birth.

This increasing familiarity with emerging life within the womb has reminded us of the phenomenal odds against the individual existence of any of us. Just consider the number of eggs awaiting release in the ovaries of the average woman, the number of sperm contained in the ejaculation of the average man and the statistical odds against any us being here, reading this, being alive, is beyond calculation. Yes, egg and sperm meet, conception takes place, new life comes about, but my life? Your life? The life of any particular person you may care to mention? The odds against that happening must be far greater than the likelihood any of us suffering a lightning strike day after day after day.

Our personal existence, our life arising at the end of this unbroken series of all these against-the-odds events, is something for which we could never express sufficient thanks. True, some lives are more manageable than others; some more bearable. Some people find life to be a series of difficult and almost impossible obstacles, but, in all this, there is, for each one of us, this individual irreplaceable existence in time and space. It is a benefit that none of us has done anything to earn, a unique circumstance over which none of us has had any control whatsoever.

Advances in medicine have significantly reduced the risks of childbirth for both mother and child. Careful monitoring during the course of a pregnancy enables the detection of potential problems at an early stage. Remedial steps can be taken to enhance the prospect of a healthy child being born to happy parents much to the relief of everyone concerned. Babies born prematurely now have a much better chance of survival than was the case in the past and instances of the death of a woman in childbirth have been progressively reduced in very many parts of the world.

All this leaves us with a sense of gratitude for having been born in this era. Undoubtedly those who come after us will benefit even more from the daily advances in pre and post-natal care and the growing knowledge of how to bring about successful outcomes in situations which were beyond recovery a very short time ago.

In a sentence or two:
Take a minute or two to realise, to really pay attention, to the extraordinary fact of your existence in this present time and place.

The Gratitude Response:
A profound "Thank You."

THE WONDERFUL WEB

Hardly anyone born since 1st January 2000 will have a recollection of the world before the internet. From tiny, tentative beginnings in 1969 internet technology has encircled the globe and opened communications on a scale previously unimagined.

As we turn on our computers and wait (impatiently) for a few seconds for Google, or some other search engine, to come up with thousands, or perhaps hundreds of thousands, of replies to our request for information, we can lose sight of the remarkable gift which is today's internet.

According to www.internetlivestats.com/internet-users, the number of internet users even as late as 1995 was only 1% of the world's population compared with nearly 40% in 2016. This fact highlights what is still a digital divide, generally between north and south, between rich and poor and between young and old. But the increasing availability of access to the World Wide Web, particularly through mobile devices, is a boon to humanity and helps in bringing about the arising of a global consciousness which can only lead to good.

Through the internet, vastly increased numbers of people have easy and instant access to information and the means of adding to their education. Even the entertainment value of the web is of importance, helping as it does to provide a vehicle by which the entire global community can experience events as one.

When human beings first set foot on the moon in 1969 hazy black and white television was the means by which an estimated 600 million people witnessed the event live. Today notwithstanding the economic and cultural differences which still keep people apart and unequal there is no doubt but that such an event if it happened today would be seen simultaneously by almost every person on earth.

In his 1922 work *Cosmogenesis* the French philosopher and Jesuit priest Pierre Teilhard de Chardin referred to the *noosphere* as a sphere of thought which he predicted would at some time encircle the earth. That prediction has indeed come true in the form of the World Wide Web.

The late Sir Arthur C. Clarke, a science fiction writer, is best known perhaps for his *2001: A Space Odyssey*. Long before it became a reality, his book *The City and the Stars* (1956) envisioned a future society, Diaspar, in which the information of the community would be accessible to all, a foretaste of what we know today as Google.

The web has opened the opportunity for a horizontal and bottom to top dissemination of ideas compared with the top to bottom process by which other hierarchical communications systems tend to operate. Anyone with an idea to share can very simply and quickly put the theory out there for the benefit of anyone who may happen to see it.

This readily available opportunity for dissemination of ideas is not without its problems, the main one being the sheer volume of information instantly available. The internet as a repository contains the good, the bad, the truth, the lies, the inspirational and the depressing. It stores the best and the worst of humanities musings. The sorting of this, the finding of truth and accuracy in an ever changing and churning mixed sea of contradictory information, creates needs for filtering, sifting and careful weighing up of the information brought to the surface. But, leaving aside all the difficulties attached to this task, it is true to say that never before have such resources been so readily available, on such a scale, to so many people, and with such ease. That phenomenon must constitute a remarkable breakthrough giving rise to endless possibilities for valuable human cooperation on a previously unthinkable planetary scale.

The web provides an opportunity for a significant number of people to co-operate effectively on enormous tasks. It facilitates co-operation in the development of medicines to enable the world to combat newly emerging diseases. It allows for the sharing of information in the fight to limit climate change. On a more personal level, it has given birth to communities of friendship through applications such as Facebook and Meetup.

The internet is beginning to merge with earlier media types such as television and radio. Applications and programs such as Skype have turned computer screens and phones into instruments that allow face to face conversation, uniting people and families living in widely separated parts of the world.

In a sentence or two:
The World Wide Web enables co-operation on a scale previously unknown and even unimagined.

The Gratitude Response:
Let all of us put this amazing facility to use for the betterment of society.

WORDS OF HUMANITY

One of the most valuable capabilities of the human race is the ability of people to speak and communicate with one another in a way which enables the thoughts of one person to be conveyed to the mind of another in considerable detail. According to www.infoplease.com, there are 6,500 spoken languages in the world as of 2016. The same source states that of these languages only about 2,000 have fewer than 1,000 speakers.

The development of language is a gift for which we must be ever grateful. Without language, civilisation as we know and enjoy it would never have developed. What is a cause for amazement is that fact that distinct groups of our ancestors developed languages by means of which they could communicate with other members of the group and which facilitated the transmission of group information and knowledge from one generation to the next.

Clearly it is impossible at this remove to formulate any strong or rational hypothesis as to how early spoken language entered the human realm. But the complexity of language has set us on a different developmental track than could have been possible with even the advanced grunts and whistles and the varied means of communication used by the various other species with whom we share the planet.

Language and the learnt ability to translate words and ideas from one language to the other have enabled members of the human race to co-operate on a global scale. Just think of the thousands of people across the world who work together on scientific research and international projects such as space exploration and the development of new medicines and new medical techniques. This cooperation helps us realise just how integrated our human race has become, due in no small measure to our ability to communicate with each other in minute detail through the gift of language.

As time goes on, there is a tendency for a small number of languages to become the dominant means of day to day and business communication for an increasing percentage of the human race. When it comes to strict business efficiency this is probably an inevitable and unstoppable trend. But in all this we need to take care. Distinct languages have evolved and developed over unimaginably long periods of time. A language contains something of the culture and thought processes of its community. We would all be the poorer if a time came about when the lesser used languages were to fall into disuse.

It is difficult to accurately convey the exact nuances of one particular language in a different language. A very simple example is the everyday English word "hello". In Gaelic, the hello greeting is the beautiful "Dia is Muire Duit" which translates as "God and Mary be with you". Of course, this arises from the Christian tradition of Ireland and it might be meaningless to someone unfamiliar with the theology which is the background to the greeting. The beautiful "Namaste" in the Hindu tradition means "I bow to the divine in you". These are far richer forms of greeting than the standard "hello" which we use in the English language or the "hi" which has crept in from the United States. The very words of a language convey something of the character and history of its people.

Language is not static. New words come into use, or into more common use, every day and dictionaries are regularly updated to keep pace with and track these changes. The names of corporations, products or programs can, through popular use, become verbs which stand in their own right and so now we can Google for facts, and we can Facetime or Skype a friend or Photoshop an image. The use of mobile devices has added a new layer of SMS language or text speak to our communications bringing us such abbreviations as the letter "c" for the word "see", "u" for "you", and much more. This trend will surely have an effect on the spelling abilities of future generations but change has always been the constant in language as in all things so presumably even the most reluctant among us will learn to adapt to new ways of expressing ourselves as our language changes.

In a sentence or two:
Do not be so enthusiastic about the drift to a few international languages for the convenience of commerce and remember and celebrate the great variety of cultures that make up the one human race.

The Gratitude Response:
Try to preserve, in everyday use at least, the spoken and written language of your own culture with all its nuances and bring that richness to bear when you use a global language for business purposes. Let us work for a unity where all will be one in terms of respect but let us also work to maintain a diversity without which we will be like peas in a pod, all very tidy but all so very, very uninteresting.

A GRATITUDE JOURNAL

There will be nothing more useful in our efforts to instil in ourselves a sense of thankfulness than the keeping of a gratitude journal. There are so many benefits reliably coming our way day by day that they can be taken for granted to the point of being sometimes entirely ignored. As a rule, it is only when we notice the absence of an everyday blessing that we come to realise just what we are missing when the benefit is lost. Only when the taken for granted advantage is withdrawn do we appreciate what we had enjoyed all along by having the previously unnoticed gift present.

A gratitude journal is a simple, powerful, beneficial remedy for helping to overcome our failure in this area. The idea is to spend some time in quiet reflection at the end of each day in grateful contemplation on some of the benefits of the day and taking note of some, perhaps as few as five, of these gifts in a systematic way. If you are undertaking this practice for the first time, it might be thought to be quite a challenging task to find five benefits for entry on the daily gratitude list. But, invariably, once you commence the project the opposite will be found to be true and you will find it difficult to limit the entries to five per day. Once we begin to think back carefully over the hours and when we recall what has happened to us in the course of the day, we will realise that we are the recipients of benefit upon benefit. We will have more than enough to report in order to get us beyond what will then be seen to be the meagre opening target of five.

The simple listing of these occasions of gratitude increases our awareness of the many good things that are part of our everyday life, advantages, kindnesses, benefits and blessings that might otherwise go unnoticed. The practice of gratitude changes our approach to life and it gives rise to even more occasions for which we can be grateful. It helps remove the demoralising idea that we are somehow entitled as of right to everything that comes to us, the idea that life owes us a living or a special living. By keeping a gratitude journal, the more we will readily notice the proliferation of our moments of happiness. The glow of that good feeling can change our lives beyond measure.

The gratitude journal can be kept in any format that facilitates ease of use. A simple notebook placed at the bedside will act as a reminder each evening that the day's entries are to be entered up. The record which is kept can be as open or as confidential as required. If confidentiality is considered especially important a system of codes and shorthand can be devised so that the notes are meaningful only to the author of the note.

For people whose preferred method is electronic rather than pen and ink, there are computer programs and smartphone apps which encourage and facilitate the easy keeping of a gratitude journal. These applications have the advantage of allowing for the generation of a nightly reminder to complete the entries of the day. They can also provide a random reminder of earlier gratitude entries and they facilitate the easy and regular recall of some of the many good things with which even the most difficult of our lives are filled.

In entering up a gratitude journal it is important not to lose sight of our regular daily blessings. The temptation might be to search back through the day seeking exceptional and extraordinary things for which to be grateful. These exceptional events indeed have an important place in our lives and when they occur they should, and probably will, give rise to feelings of thankfulness. But the smaller everyday benefits should not be neglected, nor would it be wrong or excessive to repeatedly refer to these same benefits in the journal. These are the very things, the everyday dependable things, provided by reliable people whose loyalty is never in doubt, which we can easily overlook. To our loss we take these things for granted simply by reason of their sheer unfailing reliability.

It is important too that this gratitude response would not just be an end-of-day practice. It is useful to develop the habit of paying attention to the good things of the day just as we experience them. As happy events and kindnesses arise they can be physically recorded or mentally noted for inclusion in the end of day notes.

In a sentence or two:

Gratitude is the key to happiness. But we should be grateful anyway, not simply as a means of seeking the reward of happiness, even though it is likely we will be so rewarded. We should be thankful simply because it is right to be thankful. Just as we know we should say "please", in the same way we know that it is only right that we should say "thank you".

The Gratitude Response:

See if we can maintain an awareness of the many blessing of life as we go through the day. Note anything extra special for entry in our journal at the end of the day since we do not want to overlook the special moments. But in recalling the special events, we should not lose sight of the many daily blessings which come to us from those always-reliable people who are part of our lives. The vast bulk of our lives consists of small events. To fail to notice everyday kindnesses is to miss out on quite a segment of daily gratitude and to lose out on quite a store of everyday happiness.

GRATITUDE FOR TODAY

Before rushing into the tasks of the day let us just reflect on some of the things we ought to be grateful for today.

Our very existence. This is something which is beyond understanding and an endless potential source of fascination and wonder.

Our family. Here is where we belong and where we can truly be ourselves. In a family we learn to share, to settle disputes, to try out new ideas in safety. Here is a support system based on love and continuity, our first encounter with society.

Our friends. These will perhaps be people we have known all our life, school friends and early neighbours. Our friends know us far better than we know ourselves and still they do not abandon us. For people who have never known the joy of a happy family life, true friends can be a lifeline in a sometimes scary world.

Our home. Home is a place we can return to at the end of a day, familiar surroundings, everyday people, everyday possessions. Here we don't have to put on an image to match the perceived desires of the outside world. Home is our own little corner of the world, a place where we can put our feet up and a space where we can be ourselves.

A job. Our work is a means of livelihood, a way to earn your keep. It is tragic and demoralising if we do not have a job which sustains us, a place where we can exercise our skills for the benefit of society and at the same time earn a living which will support us and the people we love. Yes, we can and we do return home exhausted at the end of a day's work but having a job and a skill is a blessing.

A belief system. By faith is not suggested a blind system of acceptance of something which is contrary to reason. It will help us if we have a considered view of the world, a view as to our place in it and our responsibility towards the people and creatures with whom we share this little oasis of life in our solar system. It is an invariable source of sadness to witness the living of an unreflective life which lacks any meaning beyond the minute to minute tasks of survival and temporary pleasure seeking. Of course by definition it is impossible for finite beings to fully grasp the nature of what may well be an eternal and infinite reality. Nevertheless the very search and exploration for meaning gives a depth to life and induces a satisfying feeling of awe. The enthusiastic living out of the questions more than compensates for the inability to find ultimate answers during the momentary flash which is the short life here of each one of us.

An absorbing hobby. This can add excitement and purpose to a life which might otherwise be full of care, hard work and even monotony. A hobby can be the attempt to learn how to play a musical instrument, paint a picture, train to run a marathon, climb a mountain. It can be working to invent something new, a project to explore some aspect of this wonderful world. The pursuit of an absorbing hobby is always something for which we can be truly grateful.

The support of society. In a thousand and one ways our existence is absolutely dependent upon the co-operation of a host of other people. An extraordinary example of this ordinary co-operation is the fact that for the most part people are not aware that their actions are contributing to this mutual support system which "just works". This working out is based upon people deciding to get up each day and setting off to work to make a living, to support their families, or to participate in unpaid activities which they enjoy. But all this semi-automatic activity is the scaffolding which keeps food on our tables, products in our shops, people offering entertainment in our cinemas, concert halls and theatres, doctors and health professionals on standby to treat our illnesses. This is an amazing example of the coming together of co-operative humanity on a quite unbelievable scale. Who could administer such a system if starting from scratch? Yet all of us have the benefit of all of this co-operation every day without having to give any of it as much as a second thought.

In a sentence or two:

Stop, look around. Everything you see is a cause for gratitude. Remember that the things you cannot see are equally beneficial, the invisible air, the inner workings of our bodies, the invisible signals coming through the air and allowing us to communicate across the planet and beyond.

The Gratitude Response:

Words fail when faced with such abundance. Let a profound "Thank You" be sufficient but remember to repeat it frequently.

PUBLIC SERVICES

We go through our days as the generally unaware recipients of public services which enable our society to function. We drive on reasonably well surfaced roads, we see a multiplicity of road signs, direction signs, traffic lights, warning signs, traffic and speed regulation signs, all erected for the safekeeping of a community of people. Where would we be without these aids, without traffic lights and speed limit warnings? Every death on our roads is one too many, an event which is devastating for the family and friends of the person lost, but can you try for a moment to imagine the danger, if not the sheer impossibility, of getting safely and conveniently from one place to another without all the aids to transport and movement which we hardly notice when they work but which we are pains to bemoan when there is a hitch affecting any of them?

We have central and local government providing a range of services for the betterment of society. Yes, there is great scope for improvement and, regardless of increased funding and the very best efforts on the part of everyone involved, there probably always will be scope for betterment. But look around and notice the supports that surround us in the fields of medicine, education, housing, opportunity and social protection, something which is not a given in every country in the world.

We enjoy the benefit of security thanks, in Ireland the UK and some other countries, to the gift of a still generally unarmed police force and we are supported by emergency services, ambulances, fire fighters, sea and mountain rescue teams, civil defence teams and members of organisations such as the Red Cross. Some of these operations are paid for through the taxation system. In other cases people volunteer their time and services unselfishly for the simple satisfaction of working for the common good.

When we need to get around by public transport we have networks of road, rail and air services all of which are the result of the co-operative work, planning and foresight of countless people living and dead. None of these services should be taken for granted. It is not a given that buses, trains and planes will be there whenever the mood takes us to make use of them. They are there only though the collaborative work of people whom we will never know but in whose debt we remain even if we seldom stop to realise the fact.

Our society is supported by a large and increasing number of voluntary organisations catering for an astonishing variety of needs. Volunteers offer help, support and guidance to young people. They promote sport, music and culture. They care for the elderly and infirm. Good Samaritans look after people with physical and mental disabilities and work to promote mental health and wellbeing. Other voluntary groups help people with literacy and numeracy problems, encourage computer literacy, care for the housebound, provide comfort for the dying. Unpaid helpers look after animals, work for tidy towns and community development, teach arts and crafts, participate in adult learning projects, help in hospitals, hospices, nursing homes and community centres. Kindly, caring volunteers counsel people who are suicidal, help with the rehabilitation of ex-prisoners, fundraise for a great variety of good causes at home and abroad, help support refugees. People give freely of their time and talents to provide assistance to the homeless, advocate for improved services from central and local government; the list goes on and on. This veritable army of volunteers acts as a positive lubricant in society, bringing people together to work for shared beneficial purposes and is something for which all of us ought to be thankful.

In a sentence or two:
We are surrounded by people, both paid people and volunteers, whose lives are dedicated to the doing of good. As we rush through our busy days we can forget these individuals and groups and the contribution they make to our wellbeing.
We notice the failures in hospitals and public services but we fail to celebrate the successes and the hard work of so many of our fellow citizens.

The Gratitude Response:
Step back, look at what you might offer to your community. Today is your opportunity to give something back by freely and voluntarily committing to deliver some service that you would love to give.

WONDERFUL DAYLIGHT

Every morning we awake to the light of a new day. There is something magical and mystical about light. The first indication of dawn triggers the singing of birds and who among us can remain unmoved at the sight of the first glow of dawn or the last rays of the setting sun?

Religions speak of light, "let there be light", "the light of Christ", "let perpetual light shine upon them". Candles and fire, candelabras and torches, have been common religious symbols throughout history. In the Christian tradition the Holy Spirit is said to have come upon the apostles of Jesus in what the gospel describe as tongues of fire. Saints and sages of all faiths are frequently depicted as having a halo of light surrounding their heads. Cemeteries and places of remembrance are often adorned with lights which are set up and fired as "eternal flames'. People of all faiths and none who claim to have had near death experiences speak of travelling through a tunnel in the direction of light.

There is something about light which speaks to a universal longing in the human soul. Is this a yearning that arises from the fact that all those billions of years ago the universe as we know it had its origin as one indescribably highly concentrated eruption of light at the time of the Big Bang? We are, all of us, after all, stardust. Whatever its basis it is clear that light is one of our fundamental comforts.

The light of the sun gives warmth and provides the energy and growth which sustains life on earth. When we observe the night sky we are in awe at the beauty of starlight. Such are the distances involved that we measure not in miles or kilometers but according to the speed of light, 186,000 miles (nearly 300,000 km) per second. At this speed the moon is only one and a half seconds away from us and the sun would be reached in 8 minutes and 18 seconds. But Proxima Centauri, the closest star to our sun is 4.35 years away even at the speed of light. Our Milky Way galaxy comprising something between 200 and 400 billion stars is 100,000 light years across. Our nearest galactic neighbour the Andromeda Galaxy is approximately 2.5 million light-years from Earth and Andromeda is only another of the believed 100 billion galaxies in the known universe. Considering this vastness and abundance we can come to more readily accept the oft quoted astonishing statement that there are more stars in the heavens than there are grains of sand on all the beaches and deserts of earth. What an amazing universe and what a cause of gratitude and wonder.

When we look up at the sky, we must remember that we are looking back in time. If the sun were to suddenly cease burning it would be 8 minutes before we would see its light go out. In the same way, when we look at the Andromeda Galaxy, we are observing its light not as it is right now but as it was more than 2 million years ago. It is a sobering reminder of this vastness to realise that when we look up at any star we could be observing light which has travelled across space for very many years after the star itself has burnt out.

Meanwhile back on earth light holds a fascination for us every day. The colours of the sky, changing minute by minute, have been and are an unending source of inspiration for artists, photographers and poets. The ever changing colours and moods of the sky in many ways reflect the changing colours, moods and life stages of each of us, the brightness of morning, the heat of midday, the quiet of evening, the rest before nightfall, clear skies, cloudy skies, troubled unsettled stormy skies, aggressive skies, peaceful skies after a storm. All of human life can be meditated upon as we look up at the ever-changing wonder that is the light we observe in the firmament above us.

In a sentence or two:
We live and move in light. Light calls us to the gift of each new day and the setting sun calls us to rest. Urban life and timetables can upset this natural balance but, wherever we are and whenever we can, we should try enter into the natural harmony that light brings to the start and to the end of every day.

The Gratitude Response:
Pay attention to the sky, notice the variation of light, enjoy the reflection of light upon water, notice the light reflected in the glass facades of the buildings of our modern cities. Pay attention to evening light, close your eyes periodically as the sun fades, open them again every so often and notice the subtle changes in colour as the light of day yields to the peace of night.

THE MAGIC OF FLIGHT

Little more than a century ago, on the 17th December 1903, in fact, Orville Wright piloted the first powered aeroplane. The pioneering craft flew just 20 feet above a wind-swept beach in North Carolina in a flight which lasted just 12 seconds. Amazingly only 66 years later men were walking on the moon.

The world's first satellite, Sputnik 1, was launched into orbit by Russia on the 4th October 1957 but today there are thousands of satellites orbiting the earth facilitating global communications, weather forecasting and providing the global positioning system which helps us find our way in traffic. We have a permanently manned International Space Station orbiting the earth and there is serious talk of a manned mission to Mars. Meanwhile, our unmanned spacecraft are reporting back with photographs and data from the outermost reaches of the solar system.

Today it is utterly commonplace for millions of people to enter metal cylinders to be whisked across the world without as much as a thought as to how completely outlandish and marvellous is this procedure.

The miracle of flight goes unnoticed, especially by frequent travellers. We complain about the tedium of air travel, the boredom of long flights, the quality of the food. We moan about shortage of legroom, the non-availability of in-flight internet access, all this as we sail above the clouds, hardly bothering to look down upon the glorious earth until we finally come to a comfortable and stress-free landing in a different country or on a different continent. How short is the memory of people?

For millennia, since humans first set eyes on birds enjoying the freedom of the air, people have dreamed of the idea of human flight. The first primitive attempts make comical viewing on YouTube today. We see brave, adventurous people attaching wing-like structures to their arms, and positioning themselves on complicated bicycle-like contraptions. These intrepid pioneers of flight take a deep breath and, heading at the greatest speed they can muster they approach a precipice in order to facilitate a brief attempt at flight before inevitably succumbing to the force of gravity, varying degrees of injury resulting as each new attempt to take to the air comes to an abrupt end.

When we look back at these early attempts at human flight, it is a source of amazement that aircraft as we know them today ever came into existence, much less into everyday use. There are as of 2016 something in the region of 100,000 flights taking off every day across the world. Just think of the air-conditioned comfort, the clockwork reliability, the ever increasing safety control systems. Consider the interconnected systems of air traffic control, the worldwide network of airports, airlines and timetables, the painstaking investigation as to the reason for each rare mishap. When we consider all this, we are in awe at how matters have progressed since humanity made its first halting attempts to take to the skies. Yes, indeed we endure the unavoidable tedium of managing to get to and through airports. We undergo the ever more detailed security checks. We note the frustrating but understandable restrictions on what otherwise would be our human tendency to bring all our possessions along with us on our every flight. But these inconveniences are a small price to pay when you consider the wonder that is our ability to join the birds of the air in the magic of flight.

In our use of air travel we need to be conscious of the impact which travelling by air has on our environment. Ours is not a planet with unlimited resources; there could hardly be such a place, and this one fragile Earth is home to all of us. The fuel needed for transport is a finite resource. The atmosphere into which we thoughtlessly pour our emissions is not capable of unlimited absorption of all the pollution we might potentially ask it to bear. Our emissions are adding to the problem of human-induced global warming. So, at the risk of appearing to be ungrateful for our fantastic flying machines and all they offer us in terms of convenience, we have to ask ourselves some questions: Is this flight reasonably necessary? Is it reasonable having regard to my obligations towards environmental stability? Is this trip being undertaken merely out of boredom or just for the fun of it? Is it something as flippant as a flying trip to Paris for lunch before flying back home for supper?

If we examine our plans mindfully, we will be guided on the right path and we can enjoy the enchantment of flight with a clear conscience.

In a sentence or two:

Pay a little more attention when you see planes passing overhead, each flight is something wonderful, the product of human ingenuity, the result of human determination to succeed and our desire to create and explore.

The Gratitude Response:

Keep a sense of awe and wonder as you fly or as you see planes in flight. Air travel is something that would have seemed miraculous to earlier generations of people. The machines passing overhead would have appeared to them as chariots of the gods as indeed, in a sense, they are.

THE WONDER OF TECHNOLOGY

Just imagine what your great grandparents would think if they were were to be whisked forward into today's world. Visualise how you would be received if you were to be taken back in time to even the beginning of the 20th century and if you had in your backpack even a fraction of the gadgets and devices which we take for granted today. Observers would treat you like a god; your remote control would be like a magic wand and your other devices would be considered to be products of some imagined heaven.

The industrial revolution brought about life-altering changes for the people who lived though that ground-breaking time. Not all the changes were positive for all individuals. For many people, the building of factories and the advent of machines turned them into mere cogs in one massive industrial system. Even today people speak about "human resources", an expression which tends to deprecate the value of the human input into industrial output. But, if we can manage to put to one side the often terrifying human cost of industrial production, we have to admit that mechanised production has indeed transformed the physical world.

Industrialisation and robotic manufacture have enabled goods to be produced on a larger scale and at an ever decreasing cost so that the living standards of huge numbers of people have improved beyond recognition. Many of the conveniences which we take for granted today would not have been enjoyed even by the wealthiest and most powerful in society in past times. Sanitation and the heating and lighting of premises are just some examples of common benefits which we enjoy today in even humble homes, comforts which were unknown even in castles and palaces a relatively short time ago.

Today the revolution continues in miniature form, electronics have utterly transformed the way in which we live. Electronics have become increasingly part of ordinary everyday objects with the size of electronic components decreasing as fast as their power is increasing. People have in their pockets and handbags electronic devices with computing power vastly beyond what was available to the scientists who worked on the ground-breaking project to send the first people to the moon in the 1960s. Who even then would have believed that the average person in the early part of the 21st century would routinely have in his or her pocket a device which would enable its owner to have access to almost all the information available to humanity? And we still complain when we happen to suffer the inconvenience of an occasional dropped signal.

Electronics have had an enormous impact on human healthcare. The simple ability to store and share health records is a significant benefit both as an aid in reducing risk and ensuring accurate, speedy access to essential personal health information. The electronics in medical equipment facilitate treatments that would otherwise be impossible. Electronics enable precise monitoring in the course of surgical operations, they allow for the possibility of robotic keyhole surgery. Thanks to electronics we can produce detained images and scans of the human body. Electronics have enabled the control of a range machines which help to keep people alive and monitored during hospital treatment. We have the benefit of a host of electronic devices in everyday use, machines which are so commonplace as to be taken for granted, tiny in-ear hearing aids, heart pacemakers inserted under the skin, electrocardiograph machines for recording the electrical activity of the heart over a period.

The so-called Internet of Things is fast becoming a reality with billions of devices expected to be created, connected and interconnected within a short number of years. The Internet of Things already enables household services and devices such as heating and lighting to be controlled and monitored remotely. But this is only the beginning. Some cars already have sensors that alert a driver, or even slow or stop a car when a hazard is detected. Google and other companies are working on driverless cars which can respond to their surroundings. Fridges will keep track of their contents and prompt us when we need to restock. The Internet of Things is not without its hazards, not least of them being security, but the ingenuity and creativity of the human race are leading us into a brave new world of possibilities for which we must overcome our reluctance to change. We need to take sensible precautions and be thankful.

In a sentence or two:
Technology, old and new, has transformed our lives, largely for the better. It has connected our world and eased our labours as never before.

The Gratitude Response:
People need to experience nature and of course, we benefit from a closer relationship to the natural world. Indeed, we should and must experience and value the great outdoors, an environment increasingly under threat from human activity. But pay attention also to the man-made environment and be grateful for the products of human ingenuity

GRATITUDE EXERCISES - 1 - LOOK AT YOUR HOME

Begin this reflection by taking a few minutes to look around your home.

Look at it with fresh eyes, the curious eyes of a child, the exploring eyes of a visitor from another place.

Notice the building that is home to you, pay attention to all of its parts.

Look up, look down, to the right, to the left, notice that it has foundations, floors, ceilings, walls, windows, doors, see its fixtures, notice its connections to the services coming in from the outside world.

Just think of all the work which has gone into the construction of this place, the materials used, the source of those materials, the people involved in the production of all that went into the making of this building, the transport involved in bringing all of the material to the site.

Think of the planning, the skill of the workers, the hours of training, the blood, the sweat and possibly even the tears involved in the course of this work. Ponder the fact that people have exchanged parts of their lives, earning a living to support themselves and their families through working to make this building so that it would become a home for you.

Your home is inextricably bound up with the work and lives of very many other people whose identity will never be known to you. Skilled craftspeople have worked to create something significant and lasting and of which they might be proud. You will have had the input of unskilled hard-working people who were trying to make a living. For those who helped in its construction, the building of this home was a blessing. It was a blessing also to the people who needed the financial support generated through the efforts of those who built it

This building is your home and more. It is the product of human co-operation, a sanctuary of your own. For you it is a place where you can centre your life and a place the creation of which has been part of the lives of so very many other people. It is a cause of happiness for you, a refuge to which you can retreat from the hustle and bustle of the world; it's very bricks a source of meditation and unending gratitude. All that is required is that you open your eyes.

May your every entry into this place be a source of happiness for you and may your every going out from it be an opportunity to extend that joy into the world

To conclude the reflection:

Now take time to sit quietly, stay in the present moment and pay attention to the place you call home.

Give thanks for Home Sweet Home.

GRATITUDE EXERCISES - 2 - BLESSINGS OF THE DAY

Begin this reflection by making sure that you are in a posture that helps meditation.

It is important to be in a comfortable position.

Your back should be straight, neither slumped nor rigid. It should be in the nature of a dignified sitting. That will help to keep you alert.

Next see if you can deliberately tense your shoulders for a second or two and then release them. This gives you an opportunity to pay attention to, and then release, the tension in the shoulders. If your shoulders can relax then perhaps you can fully relax.

For a little while just pay attention to your breathing out and your breathing in.

If you have a meditation bell you might like to sound it now and as you do so you might think of and repeat words such as the following which will help you focus on your breath:

"Breathing in I am aware that I am breathing in

Breathing out I am aware that I am breathing out."

Next just become aware of your body at rest, here and now, and bring your mind to a feeling of thankfulness for the fact that you are alive. Give thanks for your altogether unique existence.

Next recite some gratitude thoughts, mindfully pausing between each:

May I be filled with thanks for the fact that I am alive here and now.

May I be thankful for the fact that I woke up this morning.

That I had the means to get out of bed.

That I had a bed in which to sleep.

That I had a house in which to lie down.

For these blessings may I be filled with thanks.

TAKE A PAUSE FOR REFLECTION

May I be thankful for the fact that I have food to eat, clean water to drink.

May I be grateful for human society with all its supports.

For farmers who produce the food.

For factories and machines packing food and keeping it safe.

For transport people and shopkeepers who get food to me.

May I remember that every bite I eat is a gift from the whole universe, the earth in which it grows, the sun which gives it heat, the rain which waters it, the insects fertilising the plants and the hard loving work of countless people without whom life as I know it would be impossible.

For all these blessings may I be filled with thanks.

TAKE A PAUSE FOR REFLECTION

May I be thankful for the emergence of life on earth including, and especially, my own life.

May I be grateful for the benefits of civilisation, education, healthcare, transport, communications, and all the scientific advances that we take for granted but without which life would be unimaginably more challenging.

For all these many blessings may I be filled with thanks.

TAKE A PAUSE FOR REFLECTION

There are days when life seems to go against me, days when I suffer a loss of one kind or another, sometimes severe and almost unbearable loss; then there are the ordinary everyday irritations, traffic jams, people going against me. In these moments let me recall all the benefits of my life, all the things that I can and should be thankful for, and help me come back into a present moment which, when I find it, is always filled with contentment and peace.

For all the benefits of every day may I be filled with thanks.

TAKE A PAUSE FOR REFLECTION

Next make your resolution at the conclusion of this meditation:

I resolve to go out into the world through a door of hope for the future, remembering these words of Martin Luther "Even if I knew that tomorrow the world would go to pieces, I would still plant my apple tree."

So may it be.

May I be filled with loving-kindness.

May I be safe from all dangers.

May I be well in body and mind.

May I be at ease and happy.

Relax for a few minutes before sounding your closing bell and concluding your period of reflection

GRATITUDE EXERCISES - 3 - THE HUMAN BODY

The purpose of this exercise is to provide a short escape from the rush of the day, a period of mindfulness concluding with a suggested exercise to generate a feeling of gratitude for the body.

First of all, please try to get yourself into a comfortable position which facilitates quiet reflection.

If you have a meditation bell, you might like to sound it now and as you do so you might think something along the lines of the following:

"I cannot change the past but the present is my opportunity to change the future, I can live in future with an increased awareness of all my reasons for gratitude "

See if you can relax and come into an awareness of your existence in this present moment.

And just notice your breath

Become aware of your breathing in and become aware of your breathing out.

Breathing in - breathing out.

TAKE A PAUSE FOR REFLECTION

(In times of stress or worry it is helpful to remember that we can always turn our attention to the breath and come back to the present moment. Your breath is always with you. All you need do is to remember it and to make use of it.)

Next just leave aside for the following few minutes the concerns of the day, the list of jobs to be done, any worries about the past, any fears about the future. All this can wait for attention later.

This time is your time, here and now, your time of regeneration.

TAKE A PAUSE FOR REFLECTION

Allow yourself a short period of uninterrupted space where you can enjoy being here now.

If you felt yourself drifting off into thought during the last intended period of reflection don't let that worry you, at least you became aware of it. Noticing the tendency to distraction is itself an act of mindful awareness. Do do not trouble yourself if it happened, just gently return to the awareness of your breath

(In future just see if you can just gently bring yourself back to the breath. Notice how difficult it is to stay focused. Of course, that is why we call this a *practice.*)

FOLLOW UP TO TODAY'S REFLECTION:

As an exercise in gratitude for the body you might like to try this:

On your next day off work, bandage your dominant hand and put it in a sling.

Go very carefully about your business. Get dressed, unscrew a jar, unlock a door, **(no need to remind you that you should not attempt driving or cycling or undertake anything that would give rise to danger!)**

Prepare your food, eat your meals. Have a shower while at the same the time trying to keep the bandaged arm totally dry.

See if you can attempt a little one handed typing, read a book, peel an orange.

Sign a letter, put on a jacket and go out to buy the paper.

Later in the same day undo the bandage.

Look afresh for a few minutes at your taken-for-granted hand.

Express real gratitude.

Think of all the everyday blessings of a fully functioning body which we so seldom notice.

After the above, pause for a little while to give yourself an opportunity to reflect on the wonder of your human body.

Slowly work your way up from your feet to your head, paying attention to each part and noticing any sensations in each part. This is a body scan of your own. Recognise your body for the marvellous piece of engineering that it is. Be thankful for your body and for your brain which is capable of contemplating it all.

TAKE A PAUSE FOR REFLECTION

Next pause for a time to meditate in gratitude for the marvel that is your human body.

Thought to conclude your period of reflection:

During any day you will hear all types of different bells and alarms, phones ringing, bells on the TV or the radio, alarm bells, reminder bells, church bells, horns, beeps in traffic.

May every chime you hear be a reminder to you to take a mindful break - just a second or two - where you bring your attention back to the "now" and where you give thanks for the life that you enjoy in your wonderful body in that present moment.

May you remember to be mindfully present and may you enjoy the peace that you will find in each present moment.

A FINAL WORD - LOOK AROUND IN GRATITUDE

Just stop for a few minutes, look around and prepare to be moved by the extent of the benefits that surround you every day.

Give thanks to God, or goodness, or fate, or providence, or nature, or whoever, or whatever might be responsible for, or the cause of, all the countless gifts of your life.

Give thanks for the chair you sit upon, for your feet, your socks and your shoes, for the floor and the carpet, for the heating and the window and the daylight outside, for your house and your family, your neighbours and friends, your colleagues and co-operators, for the road outside and for traffic lights, the road markings and the bridges, the tunnels, the maps and the direction signs, for the shops and the shelves, the food and the provisions, the checkouts and the money, the card reader and the cashiers, for the newspapers and the magazines, for the phone, the TV and the computer, for the electricity and the energy, the clocks, the watches, the calendars and the reminders, for the holidays, the planes and the ships, the airports and the air traffic control, the seaports, the sea, the waves, the sand, for the weather and for weather forecasting, for the wind and the rain, the snow, the variety of the seasons, for the mountains and the hills, the forests and the fields, for the rivers, the lakes, the deserts, for beautiful inspiring sunrises and sunsets marking the start and end of each of our days, for the seas, the fish, the known and still unknown creatures of the deep, for fresh water and sanitation, for animals, trees and plants and for agriculture, for flowers and insects, for gardens and buildings, for hobbies and interests, pastimes and the works of our hands, for legs, hands, arms, heart and lungs and for our brain, our intelligence and skills, for the gift of memory, for music and content of books, for CDs, DVDs, MP3s, for computers, iPads and tablets, Kindles and e-readers, for the cinema and the theatre, actors, actresses, performers impresarios and entertainers, for buses and trains, for taxis and trams, for crèches, schools, colleges and universities, for teachers and professors, for philosophers, thinkers, social scientists and inventors, for surgeons, doctors and nurses, care workers and morticians, chiropodists and opticians, fitness trainers, hairdressers and beauticians, for schools of medicine, hospitals, operating theatres, for anesthetics, heart-lung machines and pacemakers, for traditional surgery and robotic surgery, for replacement hips and knees, for artificial limbs, transplants, blood transfusions, medicines and vaccines, for taken-for-granted health-enhancing devices, spectacles, walking aids, hearing aids, chairlifts, accessibility aids, for ambulances and fire brigades, for emergency workers and for international aid organisations bringing assistance in times of major disaster, for health and safety officials and pharmacists and for people who work in disease control, for dentists and their skills, for fillings, dentures, dental implants and the sedation which aids dental work, for vets and animals, for farmers, farms and farm machinery bringing food to the world, for factories, automation and machines and a host of labour-saving and production-assisting devices, for exhibitions and displays, for fireworks and festivals, floodlights and light shows, for sport and games, for stadia and sports venues, for starlight and moonlight, telescopes and microscopes, for satellites, space rockets, lunar landers and Mars rovers, for interplanetary exploration machines, for the Hubble telescope, for the moon, for the sun which gives life, for the rotation of the earth which gives us our days and the Earth's tilt giving us the seasons, for the planets and the stars, for the solar system, the galaxies, the universe itself, for the Big Bang and for black holes, for asteroids and atoms and subatomic particles, for CERN the large hadron collider, for gravity, for Einstein and Newton, for Galileo, for Marie Curie and Alan Turing, for Stephen Hawking and for countless other scientists and discoverers, for the Wright brothers and the invention of human flight, for Yuri Gagarin the first man in space, for Neil Armstrong, the first man to set foot upon the moon and for his memorable words "That's one small step for a man, one giant leap for mankind." and for all the explorers that have gone before us, for musicians and composers, for Beethoven and Bach, for Hayden and Mozart, for Handel and the Hallelujah Chorus, for Tchaikovsky and the 1812 Overture, for Liszt, Chopin and for all composers of timeless classical music that has uplifted the hearts and souls of people for centuries, for Elvis and for the Beatles, for the Rolling Stones and for Abba, for concert halls, music halls and musicals and for all the performers of popular music that has entertained people in our time, for radio and TV stations and broadcasters, for musical instruments of every description, for writers, for Shakespeare and Joyce, for Wilde and for Dostoevsky, for Hemmingway and for all writers of fiction and non-fiction who have opened and challenged the minds of people throughout the ages, for scribes of old, for the printing press, for libraries and for digital storage systems for the purpose of storing the information of humanity and carrying that wisdom forward from one generation to the next, for architects and engineers and for their buildings and creations that have enhanced the environment and improved the living conditions of people, for places devoted to meditation, recollection and prayer and for candles, lamps, incense, bells, and other aids to mindfulness, for planetary evolution and human evolution, for human society and for groups of people and nations working together in harmony, for the diversity of races and cultures sharing this planet, for democracy and the freedom to select a government, for the variety of languages, for the diversity of beliefs with which people of all ages have attempted to express their understanding of the nature of this wonderful reality in which we find ourselves, for enlightened political and moral leaders and for every person who has ever inspired anyone to be better than they might otherwise be, for environmentalists and for peacemakers, for so many people who work tirelessly to promote the common good, for individuals who lead us to better places, for those who promote freedom, tolerance and understanding, for those who work for equality, fairness, kindness, compassion, humanity and true love and for all who work to promote the virtues that help to make us truly human beings, for people who light the flame of hope and courage within us when our own flame flickers or has has gone out.

For all the numberless benefits, all the impossible-to-list people and for each and every one of our thousand and one supports in this wild and wondrous life, may we ever be truly and profoundly thankful.

And now let *your* light shine!

"At times, our own light goes out and is rekindled by a spark from another person. Each of us has cause to think with deep gratitude of those who have lighted the flame within us."

- Albert Schweitzer

About the Author

Tony Brady lives with his wife Fran, an environmental activist, in Dublin, Ireland.

His introduction to meditation in the sense that we understand it today was through the reading in 1994 of Mindfulness Meditation for Everyday Life written by Jon Kabat-Zinn.

Tony has attended retreats in Plum Village in France, a mindfulness centre founded by Zen Master Thich Nhat Hanh, Dzogchen Beara, a Tibetan Buddhist retreat centre on the Beara Peninsula in south-west Ireland, and Jampa Ling a retreat centre in the Tibetan Buddhist tradition in County Cavan, Ireland.

He founded and facilitates on-line weekly meditations through Mindfulness Meditation Dublin, a meetup group dedicated to exploring the world's ethics. He also facilitates remote on-line mindfulness sessions for widely scattered employees as required.

He contributes audio meditations and reflections to the Insight Timer Meditation App where his recordings have been listened to more than 900,000 times.

He promotes new beginnings and a life of gratitude though his website www.lifeofmindfulness.com

Also by Tony Brady

Just for Today
A guide to mindful living day by day

Simply Calling God
Reflections and prayers for life's situations

100 Words On:
Reflections for life – a simple 31 day program – in 100 word
segments

A Wave of Blessing:
Enter the wonderful world of the present moment by noticing all
you have

All the above available on Amazon

+++

May all beings be peaceful.
May all beings be happy.
May all beings be safe.
May all beings awaken to the light of their true nature.
May all beings be free.

Begin Your Gratitude Journal – People

People in your life towards whom you feel a sense of gratitude:

Begin Your Gratitude Journal – Things

Things in your life for which you feel a sense of gratitude:

Begin Your Gratitude Journal – Events

Events in your life for which you feel a sense of gratitude:

Notes – What will you do to express gratitude?

How will you give thanks for all you have received?

Let the conversation continue

Continue your exploration at www.lifeofmindfulness.com

Made in United States
North Haven, CT
19 February 2023